Lose Your Stuff Find Yourself

Break Free From Clutter's Emotional Grip

Lori Firsdon

www.ForteOrganizers.com

ISBN: 978-0-9988375-0-5

Dedication

To all of my treasured clients, who have allowed me into their homes and shared their personal challenges. It is a pleasure watching you reach individual milestones and grow in your own way.

To my wonderful family, who many times took a back seat and acted self-sufficiently, while understanding that someone in the world needed me just a bit more than they did at the moment.

TABLE OF CONTENTS

Dedication

Author's Note

Introduction

PART ONE

PART THREE

Author's Note

Dear Reader,

The chapters in this book are a collection of articles I wrote as a columnist for the Dayton Daily Newspaper.

They are designed to help you through the emotional side of getting organized. A critical first step in living a more organized life is changing your emotional response.

You must first be in the right frame of mind in order to successfully declutter and conquer the obstacles in your home. This book's focus is on the emotional responses you feel regarding your things.

Pick this book up when you need a motivational or inspirational nudge. It does not need to be read from cover to cover before you can get started.

If you read a chapter and it moves you to action, take action immediately! Don't wait until you finish reading the book. Often times, it is this action that creates the motivation needed to keep you moving toward your goals.

If you get stuck or feel paralyzed while decluttering, pick up the book again and read until you feel inspired to continue.

Find the strength you need within these pages, then be patient and forgiving of yourself in this process of personal change.

I wish you the best of luck on your journey to gain freedom from the excess stuff in your home. Even though I can't be with you in person to guide and cheer you on, know my spirit is with you every step of the way.

Love,
Lori

Introduction

The goal of this book is to get you to think differently about your things and motivate you to take action, while moving in the direction of a more organized life.

Through this process, you'll be asked to think about who you are and what you want your future to be like. You'll have tough decisions to make, but also goals that will give you the strength you need to let go and move forward.

There are so many benefits to living an organized life. In these pages, you'll discover ways to save money, gain time, acquire more space, improve your relationships and save your sanity!

Sometimes, making up your mind to allow for change takes time. As you read some of these chapters your first instinct may be to feel defensive. That's okay. Let the words sink into your consciousness and think about them as you go about your day.

If you struggle to get out the door in the morning, think about how convenient it would be to find things faster.

When you get to where you were going and you have forgotten something, think about what it would feel like to be more prepared.

If people comment on your disorganization, even in a joking manner, think about how nice it would be to not feel so self-conscious.

If it's too hard to make a nutritious meal when you arrive home, think about the advantages of having what you need at your fingertips and a clear space to work.

And when you retire for the evening, think about what a blessing it would be to wake up the next morning with less to worry about.

Letting these thoughts circulate in your mind is action. Your first step to getting organized is to come to the realization that your stuff is keeping you from the life you deserve.

Refer back to the book to gain momentum and arm yourself with the necessary tools needed to welcome change.

Mastery of your life begins with a single step.

Let's get started.

Part One

Think Differently About Stuff

In Part One, we focus on the emotional aspects of disorganization, and how your belongings can divert you from reaching your life goals.

*E*verything you own comes attached to an emotion. As you look through the items in your home, it's normal for you to feel these emotions. These items represent your history. They're relics of your life lived up to this point, so each one has a story.

The stuff we own can bring about positive feelings. We can feel blessed, calm, important, joyful, energized, loved, comforted, and happy.

Unfortunately, our things can also usher in negative reactions; such as feeling overwhelmed, paralyzed, depressed, upset, sad, ashamed, guilty, embarrassed, fatigued, and frustrated.

Think about each of your belongings and how they fit into the big picture. An item that brings about a positive feeling when first viewed can also bring up a negative feeling when you think about its overall impact.

For example, you may love clothing. As you look at each piece of clothing in your home, you feel happy, yet you own too many clothes and your home is disorganized. As a result, you feel embarrassed to have guests over, which can lead to feelings of loneliness.

A piece of clothing can bring about temporary happiness, but we're striving for long-term happiness.

As you read through each chapter, think about what long-term happiness looks like for you. Every item you own either adds value to or detracts from the life you want to lead.

It's human to feel emotions as you walk through your home. It's okay to feel these things. Let them come. Cry when you need to cry. Reminisce. Feel joy. Appreciate the items that served their purpose for you, but don't let your emotions get in the way of making the changes you need to make.

You'll discover in these upcoming chapters that items are mementoes, not memories.

Understanding the difference is important as you go through the purging process.

A memento is something tangible. It's an item you can hold in your hand, point to and tell a story about.

Memories are something you keep with you at all times. Take a minute to close your eyes and put your hand over your heart. Now think about a loved one.

Story after story comes to mind even though you aren't holding any of their belongings. You can remember them, without storing mass quantities of their possessions. Your love for them is always with you, not hidden in a box somewhere.

Again, with your hand over your heart and your eyes closed, think about a special day such as your wedding day or a special vacation. The love and excitement is there, yet you aren't holding any mementoes. You don't need your wedding dress or state shaped magnets to remember special days, especially if an abundance of these items is keeping you from loving yourself.

When you read through Part One, take time to reflect and let the feelings wash over you, while you prepare to put yourself first and your belongings second.

CHAPTER 1

Organizing Starts Before You Touch the First Thing

People often ask me where they should start when organizing their home or office. My answer is always the same: in your mind.

Going from disorganized to organized is no different than any other habit you try to break. You must first open up your mind to change.

Let's use the smoking habit as an example. You can show someone who smokes a picture of a lung blackened by the effects of smoking, share statistics as to why they should quit and point out all the drawbacks of smoking. If the person is not ready to quit, all of these facts will not be seen or heard.

It's not until the person makes up his own mind, in his own time, to quit smoking that these facts become tools needed to gain the power to quit.

> "Once a person is determined to help themselves, there is nothing that can stop them."
>
> ~Nelson Mandela

The change from being disorganized to being organized works the same way as quitting smoking. It's not until you make up your own mind, in your own time, that you will be successful at getting more organized.

I can give you a list of benefits of being organized, share with you the health risks associated with disorganization and show you testimonials from others who are newly organized. However, if you're not ready to change, you will find excuses and become defensive when these facts are presented.

So how can you make up your mind to get more organized when you know deep down this would be good for you?

Focus on your future. If you're tired of wasting your spare time on stuff you don't use and have had enough of playing the "rearranging my things game," you need to think about what you want to do with the rest of your life.

Start by writing down three goals you would like to achieve. They can be personal, work-related or a combination of the two.

I've had clients who get stumped at this step. Life has got them down and they tell me they don't have any goals. Everyone has goals. You are just trying to think too big, which is making this step more difficult.

Instead, think of smaller goals to help you figure out what you want the next chapter of your life to look like.

Think about which people in your life energize you and make you feel good about yourself. A goal could be to spend more time with your family, friends, clients or volunteering to help someone in need.

Decide on something you want to get better at. Do you want to learn how to dance, make your own wine or become a better cook?

For another goal, focus on what makes you happy. For me that would be a long weekend camping with my family. For you that might mean joining an adult soccer league or reading a novel in your favorite chair. What makes you happy?

Now use these goals to help you make up your mind that getting organized will be beneficial for you.

Whenever you get stumped about letting something go, ask, "How will this item help me reach my goals?"

When your mind is made up that being more organized will help you reach your goals, you won't let stuff get in your way.

CHAPTER 2

The Cost of Keeping Things

For many of you getting organized is on your list of New Year's resolutions. Right up there with losing weight, saving money and exercising.

Getting organized was on your list last year, but it didn't get done. Why not?

One reason may be because you didn't change your thinking before you tried changing your behavior. You need to think differently about your stuff in order to make changes. For every item in your home, start asking yourself, "What is this item costing me?" And then ask, "Is it worth it?"

The first thing every item in your home is costing you is space. You bring items into your home and they accumulate everywhere. You buy organizing bins to help contain the piles of stuff. You continue to get more items and more organizing bins. You then purchase shelves to put these bins on. You do this over and over, and before you know it many rooms in your home are filled with boxes of stuff.

You have so many things that it's hard to find what you need. You purchase more items even though you already have them at home somewhere. Now you're spending money on new items just because you can't find what you need. This starts a vicious cycle of buying and storing. It costs you money and space in your home.

Now the stuff is costing you money to keep it. You need bins, shelves, and suddenly your home isn't big enough to hold everything. You add rooms to your existing home or buy a bigger home. If that's not possible, you build storage sheds or rent storage units to store your items off-site.

Keep in mind the free items people give you will also cost you space and money. It's so easy to bring these free things into your home if you don't think about these costs.

What is your time worth? All this stuff is costing you time. You spend time buying it and storing it. It takes time to look through it, sort it, move it around, box it up, label it, fix it and maintain it. You spend so much time dealing with the stuff you don't have time to spend on the things that are important to you.

> "A good system shortens the road to a goal."
>
> ~O.S. Marden

Everything in your home is costing space, money and time. This year, you need to go through your home room by room, item by item and make sure the items you are keeping are worth it.

Are they helping you reach your goals for this year? If not, you have so much to gain by letting them go.

Once you start thinking differently about your stuff, you will be much more successful in your organizing efforts. And once you reach your goal to be organized, your other goals will become easier. You'll have more space, money and time to pursue your other New Year's Resolutions. What a gift to give yourself this year.

CHAPTER 3

You Can't Treasure Everything

Too much of something and it is no longer special.

When I reach for a cereal spoon in the morning, it reminds me of when my children were younger and a certain spoon caused more fights than I care to remember.

Somehow, a regular, nothing-special-about-it spoon showed up in our home, mysteriously. I added it to the rest of the spoons in our drawer, even though it didn't match the others.

One of my children named it the "special spoon" and chose it over the other spoons for her breakfast. Her siblings quickly caught on that she always chose the "special spoon" and insisted we take turns.

From that moment on, our mornings were under the spell of the spoon. My children would rush to be the first in the kitchen, snapping up the spoon so they could use it. Tears and howls from the others invariably ensued. I would review the week, recap who had it last and whose turn it was next.

Sometimes one child would wait to eat breakfast until his sibling was done, so I could wash the spoon and give it to him. Other times I was so fed up that I declared no one was getting the spoon that day.

> **"Too much of something, and nothing gets treasured."**
>
> ~Unknown

If you experience these same kinds of sibling battles, then you can understand the joy I felt on the day I saw our "special spoon" for sale during a shopping trip.

I snatched up a handful of "special spoons" and couldn't wait until the next morning, knowing

14

our morning brawl was finally over.

I didn't tell the children about the new spoons. Instead, when the first child came downstairs for breakfast, I said, "Here's the special spoon. If you want to keep it, don't mention you have it to the others."

The next child entered the kitchen. Before he could get to the table, I handed him another "special spoon" and put my finger to my lips whispering, "Shhh."

Each child was now happily eating breakfast, both thinking they were the only ones with the "special spoon." This same scenario went on for days until one morning the jig was up. They discovered we had many "special spoons."

From that day on, no one cared about which spoon they got. There were so many "special spoons" that they were no longer "special" and therefore no longer treasured.

I learned a very valuable lesson that day. When the quantity of what we own is limited, things are treasured more.

Think about the items in your home. Do you

have collections that have gotten out of control? Instead of enjoying them, have they become a burden? Or have you collected so many that you don't even pay attention to them any longer?

Even good stuff; like photos, school projects, vacation souvenirs, inherited items and childhood collections, often gets thrown in boxes and stored, because you are trying to save everything instead of only the really special ones.

Like the spoon that lost its "special," so will your items if you keep everything. Saving the special ones allows you to enjoy or display them, instead of piling them up. Treasures should be cherished, not boxed up and forgotten.

CHAPTER 4

Let Go of Clutter
So You Can Relax

For Mother's Day weekend, I got to sit down and read a book without feeling guilty. I also napped when I felt sleepy, hiked with my dog, played cards with my kids and chatted with my husband around a campfire.

We spent the perfect weekend at a campground.

For me to have this perfect weekend, I first had to take this advice from a quote by Ben Stein, "The first step to getting the things you want out of life is this: decide what you want."

Take a minute now and close your eyes. Think about what a perfect weekend would be for you. What experiences do you want, who would you spend time with, what would make you happy?

> "The first step to getting the things you want out of life is this: decide what you want."
>
> ~Ben Stein

Open your eyes and keep that perfect weekend in your mind. Now, walk around your home and look for items you've been storing, but no longer need.

If you start looking at your unused items with new eyes and seeing them as things that keep you from enjoying your perfect weekend, it will be easier to part with them.

I've had to let go of many things that were important to me; the cradle my five children slept in, the saddle I used throughout my 4-H days and many of my parents' belongings after they passed.

I was able to let go of these things because none of them were helping me get to the campground.

By eliminating unneeded items in my home, I have time to enjoy all the simple things I love to do.

During the weekend my youngest daughter said, "I feel like only nice people go camping." I looked around at our fellow campers and knew why she would think that. Everyone was relaxed and enjoying their family and friends, all while having fewer belongings in tow.

What things are you holding on to that just take up your time? Many of these things need to be cleaned, maintained, organized and cost money to store. No wonder you never have time to enjoy your perfect weekend.

It's time you put a stop to storing things and start having perfect weekends. Owning fewer things will allow you to do just that.

Imagine doing what you enjoy in a very relaxed and unhurried manner. Now make it a reality. As you sort through your belongings, ask yourself this question, "How will keeping this item allow me to have my perfect weekend?"

If you see me at the campground, stop by for a visit. I'll have plenty of time to chat.

CHAPTER 5

Life Lessons from Man's Best Friend

My dog is the smart one around here.

As I pull into my driveway, I'm greeted by my dog. Her eyes watch for my car to stop and her tail wags in sweet anticipation of my car door opening. Before I can get out, she puts her head in my lap, looks up with big brown eyes and wags her tail. She is that excited to see me.

She's not looking to see if I brought her something, doesn't care what I'm wearing or what kind of car I'm driving. She just wants to see me.

She always greets my children in a like manner. As they come down the stairs in the morning, she meets them with great enthusiasm, even though the only thing they ever give her is a pat on the head.

This makes me stop to think, what do I do when my children come down the stairs first thing in the morning?

> "Life is more about who is next to you and less about what is next to you."
>
> ~Unknown

She's doesn't become jealous or bothered by the fact that others might have more than her. She has everything she needs, in us.

My dog has figured out that relationships are more important than things.

This causes me to step back and ponder. Can my dog teach me how to be happier and appreciate those around me?

My dog has few material things: a couple of toys, a leash and pillow to sleep on. But even these things don't make her happy unless I'm included with them.

She doesn't play with her toys unless I'm playing with her. The leash is not exciting unless I'm on the other end of it. And she only sleeps on the pillow, if I'm in the room where the pillow is.

When we do go for a walk and encounter another dog, she's not looking to see if the other dog has a designer collar, she just wants a friend.

If we moved to a smaller house, she wouldn't care. In fact, she would be just as happy if I pitched a tent in the backyard and invited her in. She just wants to be close to me. I make her happy, regardless of the stuff that surrounds us.

So, my dog has taught me something. The material things in my life should have a lot less value to me than the people in my life.

Life is more about who is next to you and less about what is next to you.

I need to worry more about developing relationships and spending time with my loved ones, and less about accumulating things.

Unfortunately, my dog will pass someday.

I won't keep any of her belongings. She has taught me that extra things like this just pile up and get in my way. It's her memory that I will keep with me.

She is beside me now on her pillow as I write this article. I look down at her and think, how could a mutt from the pound be so smart about life?

Thank you Heidi for reminding me...Life is for loving, not for having.

CHAPTER 6

Get More Done by Letting Go

When I share with someone that I am a professional organizer, they automatically assume I am a perfectionist. They hide their purse behind their back so I can't peek inside, or ask me to drive so I don't see the interior of their car. They would never dream of inviting me into their home as a guest. They assume that everything in my life is perfect, and therefore I would judge them in some way because their spaces aren't perfect.

They're surprised when I tell them that I don't even strive to be a perfectionist. Truth be told, I would love for everything to be in its rightful place at all times, but that's not realistic. The reality is I have never met a happy perfectionist, and being happy is a very big goal of mine.

It's impossible to be perfect in everything you do, yet many of you are trying to do just that. When I see this happening with clients I ask, "Do you consider yourself to be a perfectionist?" The reply I most often get is, "Yes, but you would never know it by looking around at how disorganized my home is." Their perfectionism is the very thing that is keeping them from getting organized.

If your home is disorganized, your perfectionism may be holding you back. Perfectionists often don't start a project unless it can be done perfectly. You focus on the perfect ending. This becomes intimidating

> **"Strive for progress, not perfection."**
>
> **~Unknown**

and you fear not doing it right, so you don't start the project at all. This fear becomes paralyzing, so nothing gets done.

Perfectionists often won't start a project unless they can complete it from start to finish without interruption. In our world of constant interruptions, this is usually impossible. So now your projects don't get started.

You can't do it perfectly, so you don't start. You don't start and nothing gets done. When this cycle continues you fall behind. You fall so far behind you become overwhelmed. Your spaces become cluttered. You get in so deep that you feel paralyzed and don't know where to begin.

Your personality wants everything around you to be perfect and yet nothing is.

This is where unhappiness and depression can set in. You feel ashamed and embarrassed, and start pushing others away.

If you have others living with you, many times your perfectionism is affecting your relationships with them. You often act irritable towards them. They begin to feel bad or fight back, because being perfect all the time is impossible for them as well.

If perfectionism is holding you back from an organized home and damaging the relationships with those you love, you need to break the perfectionist habit and believe that it's more important to be happy than perfect.

What you want to strive for is a home that is just organized enough. Just organized enough to find what you need when you need it. A home that is easy to clean. A home where family members can relax and feel peaceful.

If being organized is a goal of yours, let go of perfectionism. Get your spaces just organized enough and be happy instead of frustrated all the time.

CHAPTER 7

An Organized House Can Take the Unexpected in Stride

I recently went to Florida to visit a friend. When I envisioned the trip, I thought of warm weather, walks on the beach and returning home with a tan.

Unfortunately, the weather was cool, our walks were traded for long talks indoors, and instead of a tan I came back with the flu.

My trip lasted five days. Upon my return, my husband counted on me to share in the family responsibilities once again. My children looked forward to home cooked meals.

That was the plan until sometime during my trip home I started feeling ill. When I arrived home, I went straight to our guest bedroom and collapsed in the recliner. This is where I would spend the next ten days.

So I could hear the happenings of the house, I left the door of the room I was squirreled away in open day and night.

In the morning, alarms went off, people crisscrossed each other in the hallway, dishes clanged in the kitchen and then all would go quiet when everyone left.

"Good order is the foundation of all things."

~Edmund Burke

Later in the day, I heard after school snacks being prepared, printers spitting out homework, sports gear being gathered and the car leaving the driveway.

When they returned, there was talk around the dinner table, showers being taken and then all was quiet until the morning routine started up again.

During my illness, I marveled over the fact that they didn't need my help at all for those ten days. In fact, they helped me. They delivered meals to my door and checked on me as they passed my room.

If you were unexpectedly out of commission for ten days, how would your family manage?

If this thought panics you, then it's time you get organized before a hardship happens. One of the reasons my family managed so well without me is because having an organized home is a priority of mine. I stage my home to function without me.

We change throughout our lives and our stuff has to change with us. Too many of you are holding on to things because you're emotionally attached. Yet, your everyday life is hectic and you're not prepared for the unexpected.

I know firsthand how difficult it is to let go of things, but if you make organizing a priority you will find the strength to let go.

Stop keeping things because of who gave them to you, how much they cost, how often you once needed them or because you may need them someday.

Letting go of these items in my life allowed me to plan a trip with my girlfriend and then recover from the flu without my home becoming chaotic. There is a real freedom that comes with letting go of excess things.

My family did not have to trip over or take care of unnecessary items during my absence. This made it easier for them to find what they did need, which allowed me time to recover peacefully.

Being out of service reminded me how important it is to keep my home organized. Do yourself and your family a favor. Make organizing your home a top priority this year, so you can relax a little when things go wrong.

CHAPTER 8

Anchors That Hold You Back

Organizing our homes should be easy.

Step 1: Figure out what we want to do with the time we have remaining in this life.

Step 2: Surround ourselves with those things that support this mission.

Unfortunately for many of you, getting organized is very difficult. There are so many emotions attached to your possessions that it's hard to part with them, even when this stuff keeps you from doing the things you love to do.

When I work with people in their homes, before we ever move any of their things, I always ask, "What are your goals for the future?"

In the many years I have been a professional organizer, no one has ever responded, "Well, I want to spend my time rearranging my things, moving them from room to room, boxing them up and stacking them around my house."

Yet, many of you are doing just that. Instead of traveling, reading for pleasure, enjoying your favorite hobby or spending time with family and friends, you are spending the precious time you have left moving things around.

> **"Get rid of things, or you'll spend your whole life tidying up."**
>
> ~Marguerite Duras

Ask yourself, "Why am I taking my time to maintain, stack and trip over items that I no longer use? Why do I allow this excess stuff to take up space in my home and create additional work for me?"

Take a walk through your home. Instead of letting all the emotions you normally attach to your stuff come out, I want you to start seeing the excess items in your home as anchors. These anchors weigh you down and take up the valuable time you have left.

This simple shift in your thinking may help you part with the things you no longer need. No matter how important they were to you.

In fact, if you think about dragging these anchors behind you as you are trying to reach for what's important, you may not be able to get rid of them fast enough.

The other day I was helping a family organize their garage. The day was very hot. They had their two small children to look after while we worked.

About an hour into our time together, I looked at each of them. Mom and Dad were sweating and frustrated, because their children kept interrupting them. Their children were upset and whining, because Mom and Dad weren't able to give them their full attention.

I asked the couple, "Would you rather be at the pool right now as a family or standing in this hot garage with me?"

The obvious answer was they wanted to ditch me and head to the pool.

I replied, "Remember your choice while we work. Let's get serious about parting with as much as you can today so we won't have to spend another hot day sorting through your garage."

For the rest of the afternoon when they got stuck on an item, I simply had to say, "Pool or organizing your garage?"

Luckily for me, I never took my clients' choice personally.

CHAPTER 9

Our Stuff Creates a Host of Emotions

I just closed the novel I've been reading. The story took place during World War I. There were many injustices committed during the War. One of those was the looting and theft of people's personal belongings.

While reading through the chapters, I couldn't help noticing how many times people placed their emotions on material things.

A woman's portrait is the focus of the book. Its original owners enjoyed it immensely. For others who later owned it, it caused jealousy, resentment, fear, grief, suspicion and greed.

One chapter described how many of the residents in a town overtaken by soldiers hid as many of their belongings as possible, so they would not be stolen.

One afternoon, a grandfather clock was heard chiming. A neighbor confessed to burying some of his belongings, including the grandfather clock, so they wouldn't be taken.

The clock chimed every hour and could be heard clearly, even though it was underground. The townspeople grew afraid that it would be discovered and knew severe punishments would follow.

Their stuff became so important to them that they risked severe punishment, even death, to keep it safe.

Later in the book, some of the residents were being marched off to camps. Many of the people took their family heirlooms and other valuables with them. Their possessions were heavy and awkward, but they kept carrying them despite their starvation and exhaustion.

Instead of taking care of their personal needs and saving their energy during their journey, they wrestled with belongings. Once they reached the camps, these belongings were usually confiscated. I'm sure many realized in retrospect that they should have been holding their loved ones' hands during their walk, instead of their candelabras.

I'm not saying our stuff shouldn't be important, but what risks should we take to protect it? What emotional costs are you willing to pay for your stuff?

> "Other things may change us, but we start and end with family."
>
> ~Anthony Brandt

In modern times, I see people place such importance on their stuff that they risk their family's health and happiness.

I see homes filled with so much stuff that it harbors great amounts of dust, mold, insect infestations and even rodents. All of which cause health issues for anyone, including pets, who live in the home.

Talk to any estate attorney, estate sale planner or organizer, and you'll hear many stories of how stuff has caused emotional pain and the separation of family members.

We need to stop wasting time and emotional energy on stuff, and focus more on those we love. Anthony Brandt's quote, "Other things may change us, but we start and end with family" reminds me not to place so much importance on the stuff I own. Instead, I value time spent with friends and loved ones.

Our stuff is important to us, but we have to decide at what cost. Some costs just aren't worth it.

You can't take it with you when you pass, but it can cause much grief for family members once you're gone. How much time and energy do you want to spend on your belongings while you're alive and well?

CHAPTER 10

Does More Stuff Really Make Us Happier?

A big part of getting organized is parting with items we no longer use. Of course, this is much easier said than done. From firsthand experience, the people who let go of clutter are happier than those who hang onto everything.

So why do we hold on to so much stuff?

We often don't want to part with something because we spent a lot of money on it, even though holding onto these items doesn't get your money back. Look around your home and see what items you are keeping just because you spent a lot of money on them. Is it the American Girl doll your daughter no longer plays with, a fur coat that's not worn or a piano no one plays?

Offer these items up for sale, or donate them and get a tax deduction. You'll have a little extra spending money and more space in your home. Unused, expensive items will no longer weigh on your conscience.

Another reason we hang on to an item is because someone else gave it to us. We don't want to seem unappreciative and possibly hurt the other person's feelings by parting with it.

> "Happiness is more likely to come from people and experiences rather than things."
>
> ~Unknown

Although you may feel guilty for letting them go, these things are costing you space in your home and may be keeping you from enjoying the things you do treasure. It's okay to want your home arranged according to your own tastes and interests.

Sometimes that means parting with those things other people have given you. If you did not ask for the item, the other person guessed whether you would like it, but unfortunately they were wrong.

By keeping these items, you are training the other person to continue to give you similar things in the future. It's time to break this cycle by telling the person your tastes have changed and you no longer wish to receive these kinds of gifts.

If they insist on buying you something, steer them towards something you do need.

Finally, people are storing things in their home just because they've owned them for a long time. Ask yourself when coming across these items, "Did this item serve its purpose?"

Once you realize the item served its purpose, you may feel okay parting with it now. By letting these items go, you'll have more room in your home to enjoy the things you need in your present life.

Excess stuff doesn't bring happiness, but experiences do. Make time to part with these unnecessary items so you can have more time doing the things you love, whether it's going to a movie with friends, volunteering at your child's school or learning a new hobby.

CHAPTER 11

Why Store Things We Don't Use?

I worked with a woman who recently got divorced. We organized and reduced her belongings so she could quickly get settled into her new home.

While working in her basement, we discovered her wedding dress. It had been preserved by a company soon after her wedding.

She smiled and said, "I guess that can go now." As I was taking it away she said, "Wait, should I open it and look at it one last time?"

I smiled and said, "Only if you're curious to see if it's really in here."

She got a puzzled look on her face. Cleary, she had never heard of the wedding dress cleaning scam.

Years ago, it was discovered that companies, who were supposed to be preserving wedding dresses, were actually selling the dresses and then handing over weighted boxes without the dress.

The scammers told brides, "Once you open the box, your dress will no longer be preserved." Brides rarely opened their boxes, which is why the crime went undetected. Years later, if they discovered the box was empty, the scammers were long gone.

> "We must let go of the life we had planned so as to have the life that is waiting for us."
>
> ~Joseph Campbell

My client chose to donate her dress without opening the box. In hindsight, she wished she had sold the dress while it was still in style. She could have used that money, plus the money spent to preserve it, on something she needed at the time.

She held onto her dress to serve as a memory of her special day. But the dress was really just a memento, not the memory itself. Even with the dress truly gone, she was able to reminisce about her wedding.

Ironically, it really didn't matter if her dress was inside the box or not. She only thought she needed it.

How many of you have something taking up space in your home that you never look at?

Are you holding on to things just because you have the room to store them?

If you're feeling overwhelmed and stressed because you own too many things, stop saving things you no longer need. Let someone else benefit from items that served a purpose in your life.

You'll feel better with fewer things to take care of. Plus, your item can be purposeful again and can help make a memory for someone else.

CHAPTER 12

Choose a Few Useful Items from Loved Ones to Keep Down Clutter

Parting with our own items to live a more clutter-free life can be difficult, but parting with the belongings of a loved one who has passed away can be especially difficult. Although you may want to hold on to some of their belongings, keeping too many of them may start to affect your life in negative ways.

As an organizer working in other people's homes, I often see how people are living a stressed and cluttered life because they can't part with a deceased loved one's belongings.

One client who lost both her parents brought most of their possessions from their home into hers. The items were piled so high in the garage she could no longer park her car in there.

Among her father's belongings were many musical instruments. Since I knew she didn't play any instruments I asked, "If your dad were still living, do you think he would enjoy seeing his instruments played by someone who might not be able to afford one?" Her reply, "He would love nothing more."

In the end, she refinished her father's violin and kept in her home as a décor piece. She donated the rest of the instruments to a school to help students in need get involved in a music program.

I, too, have lost both of my parents. I decided right from the start that I would take only those items I could make use of

> **"Dig deep for your memories, but remember, the ones that really matter cannot be found in the old trunk in the attic."**
>
> **~Rosita Perez**

in my everyday life. From my mother, I kept the mixing bowl I used when making cookies as a child. As I watch my children use her bowl to make cookies, I feel like she is in the kitchen with us. From my father, I saved a handful of tools that I use on a regular basis around my home. When I use his tools to fix things today, I remember his patience as I followed him around the house and watched him make home repairs.

If you try to keep everything inherited from loved ones, your life may be impacted in negative ways. Your relationship with your spouse may be stressed because maybe it's their car not getting parked in the garage. It also takes time to clean and maintain these extra items. Their collections may be keeping you from creating that craft room you would enjoy.

When going through your deceased loved one's belongings, remember these items are mementos, not the memory. You can still remember many good times with this person without the physical items. You will treasure their items more if you keep only the best reminders of your loved ones.

CHAPTER 13

What Makes You Happy?

There was a time in my life when I couldn't have written these articles. Even though I have been an organized person as far back as I can remember, I went through a stage in my life when I thought material things brought happiness.

I am sharing my past with you in hopes that you can dodge some of my mistakes and take a shortcut to happiness.

I married at a very young age, right out of high school. With a dual income and no children, we were able to buy items without giving it much thought. We bought a home, expensive cars and a boat, just to name a few.

As the years went by, I started feeling disconnected from my husband. I shared this with him. Instead of giving me his time that I craved, he started buying me things: a fur coat, expensive jewelry and clothes. Each time they made me happy, but only for a little while.

> "It's not how much you have but what you enjoy that makes you happy."
>
> ~Unknown

As I matured, I realized that some of these material possessions were not even in line with my values. I'm an animal lover, so what was I doing with a fur coat? I feel security when saving money, yet I was driving a car whose payment exceeded my monthly mortgage payment?

I owned a horse, which required grooming a muddy animal and cleaning stalls. Expensive jewelry didn't quite fit with my hobby.

I was taking care of things that no longer brought me joy. Each year I winterized a boat that I didn't enjoy because it gave me so many problems throughout the summer.

I paid for insurance on jewelry I rarely wore and a house payment on a home where I felt lonely.

My unhappiness led to the end of my marriage. Although it was painful, I learned an incredible lesson that we hear all the time, and I now believe. Money cannot buy happiness. I realized that once my basic needs are met, spending time with a loved one is more important than material possessions.

Fast forward. I remarried over 25 years ago, and we are blessed with five children. I have a job I'm passionate about that allows me to improve other people's lives, which is incredibly rewarding.

For years, I drove an older car. I was thrilled each time I turned the key and it started. I cherish my wedding ring, so I don't need any other expensive pieces of jewelry. Our house is perfect for our family's size. If it were bigger, I would spend my time cleaning instead of enjoying family time.

When people ask me what my husband bought me for Christmas, I say, "Absolutely nothing," with a smile on my face. I value the time we spend together as a family more than material possessions.

I am far from being a minimalist, but the things I purchase are in line with my values and help me reach my goals.

Make sure the items you own match your value system and bring you real happiness.

Summary

Create Your Own Goals

After reading through the first part of this book, do you have a clearer picture of who you are at this moment? Of who you want to become moving forward? Write down some goals to help you stay focused on what's important to you.

As you walk through your home remember everything you own costs you something. Space, money, time or a combination of these. Even free stuff. Every item needs to be worth these costs.

Dealing with excessive stuff also takes emotional energy. Save items you use or display. Treasured items are enjoyed, not stuffed in a box somewhere.

Use the list of emotions mentioned in Part One to help put into words how every item you own makes you feel.

If you come across something that brings up an unpleasant emotion, give serious consideration to letting it go immediately. Why would you keep something that makes you feel bad or upsets you?

If you want to have perfect weekends, build relationships and enjoy experiences. Let go of perfectionism. It's a habit you can break.

Organize when you're not in the midst of a crisis. You'll be better prepared to deal with unexpected situations when they happen.

When you pay attention to your personal value system, it reminds you of what's really important.

Organizing is about self-love. You deserve to be happy. Let go of the things that are keeping you from true happiness.

Part Two

Let Go of Clutter

Now that you've had a chance to work on the emotional process needed to free yourself from clutter, let's continue with the organizing process.

D isorganization is sometimes caused by habits. In this next section, we explore ways to break habits that are no longer self-serving.

Some chapters speak to the habits of gift-giving, while others address the endless rearranging and storing of clutter that has become a source of frustration instead of bringing joy.

We'll touch upon how excessive belongings affect us and our relationships with loved ones. Learn to fill your home with love, not things.

Find the courage needed to start making your home a happier and safer place to be.

CHAPTER 14

Travel Light in Life

I wrote this article while sitting on the deck of a cruise ship. I was hired by their program director to teach organizing classes as part of their enrichment program.

I was a bit skeptical about people aboard a cruise ship stopping their festivities to attend seminars on how to organize their home. To my surprise, the conference room filled up with vacationers eager to learn new ways to tackle their clutter.

If people are attending classes during their vacation to learn how to deal with the excess they have created in their homes, it's time to take a serious look at what we're keeping.

I asked them, "How many of you are having a great week?" All the hands in the room shot up, while smiles and laughter filled the room.

They were happy, yet they had few belongings with them. This made me wonder, what can we learn from this?

If you start thinking like a vacationer, only keeping what you use and what adds value to your life in the present, you could travel light and be happier. By traveling light, you could pick up and go when opportunities present themselves.

What we say makes us happy and what actually makes us happy can be two different things. There are many items in our homes which we overvalue emotionally. We don't enjoy them like we thought we would. We hold onto them because we believe we will enjoy them some day.

Books – People store books even though they have little time to read. Books are heavy, take up lots of space and need dusting. Paring down your collection might actually free up more time for you to read.

Craft items – Your craft rooms are filled with items you found on sale, leftovers from past projects or supplies you might need someday. The room is now so cluttered you can't find what you need and you no longer have room to work. Surplus craft items can actually keep you from working on new projects.

Entertainment media – You have a collection of record albums, but no turntable. A library of movies, but no time to watch them. A collection of CDs, even though you use your iPod. You keep these items because someday you are going to do something with them, but in reality you just store them and allow them to be in your way.

> "Your home is living space, not storage space."
>
> ~Francine Jay

Photos – You say photos are important to you, yet they are thrown in drawers around your home and boxed up with the other clutter in your storage areas.

You don't enjoy them, because they are disorganized and the thought of tackling this project is nauseating. Pare down to a manageable amount of photos, and you will treasure them instead of just storing them.

Other extras you may need to part with – memorabilia, electronic files, magazines articles, paperwork and souvenirs. Are these items adding real value to your life or are they just keeping you busy?

I know first-hand how hard it is to let go of things. I'm not asking you to part with any of these items if you truly enjoy them. Let go of 'someday' items so you can enjoy living in the present moment.

As you let go, focus on what you are gaining instead of what you're losing. Gaining more vacation time sounds great to me.

CHAPTER 15

Action is the Only Remedy for Fear

While driving home from vacation, my husband noticed our gas gauge was dangerously low. In an instant, I saw fear overtaking him. He sat more upright, his body tensed and he appeared agitated.

To ease the tension I said, "Calm down, (spouses love when you say that), the worst thing that can happen is we run out of gas."

Our options for the worst case scenario were to walk,

call for help or ride the bikes we had with us to the gas station. Although inconvenient, nothing we couldn't manage.

When I become fearful, I have trained myself over the years to ask, "What's the worst thing that could happen?" My answer usually calms me down.

I have found that a lot of my clients were not getting organized because they let fear paralyze them.

One of my clients experienced the typical fears disorganized people can go through.

When she called me for the first time, she said, "I have known about your services for years, but was afraid to call."

> **"Do what you fear and fear disappears."**
>
> ~David Schwartz

I'm glad she called. Before hanging up, she said, "I feel so much better after talking with you. I feel like I have hope."

When I arrived at her home, she met me at my car. My years of working as an organizer told me she was afraid to let me inside and needed assurance at the curb.

I'm happy she let me in. She found me to be compassionate, understanding and ready to tackle the project.

She was afraid to get started because she had tried other times and didn't make much progress. I assured her that once we got started she would know how to continue.

We began in a room I knew would be easy for her. While organizing, she talked about how she was afraid to tackle other rooms, because items there had more sentimental value. When we eventually worked in those other rooms, I didn't have to comfort and coach her any more than I did in the first room.

One day, she met me at the door in tears, "I let go of a game that belonged to my (grown) son. When I asked my daughter about it she told me he would have wanted that game.

She was afraid to continue for fear she would keep making mistakes.

Later while talking with her son, she broke down

crying. Her son said, "Mom you're being silly, getting rid of the game was no big deal."

She was also afraid we couldn't work together without her husband present. We now have more sessions without him. In fact, she likes surprising him with the progress we make.

When she found out I sometimes organize homes when my clients are not present, she said, "I would be afraid to have you do that." She was able to overcome that fear too. I had several solo sessions working in her home.

If you have been afraid to get organized, take a minute to reread this article and notice how many times my client was afraid when she didn't need to be.

When fear keeps you from getting organized, you just have to start. Don't deliberate, over-think or try to rationalize. Just act.

By the way, we made it to the gas station. Thank goodness I didn't waste time worrying about it.

CHAPTER 16

Create Your Ideal Shack in the Space You Have

You may be in the habit of keeping things in your home without really giving much thought as to why you are keeping them. What would your life be like if you could get out of this habit of keeping things you don't need?

I worked with a client who is a writer and has a home office. As he described the things in his office, I got the impression that the items he surrounded himself with were more of a comfort than useful. He had books he had read, yet would never read again. Many books he wanted to read, but he admitted he would never get to them.

There were papers he had written, along with the notes used to create them.

I asked him where the notes were that he would need for future writing projects. He buried his head in his hands and said, "Somewhere in here, everything is mixed together."

He was frustrated and worried, because of his age, he knew he had limited time to accomplish the writing projects that were important to him. I saw the stress this caused him and wanted to help him reach his writing goals.

> "It's in the things we lose that we discover what we most treasure."
>
> ~Adriana Trigiani

I pointed out that most of the items in his office actually distracted him from his work. I then asked him what his perfect 'creative space' would be. He said, "I would build a shack in my backyard and I would only keep the things I need to finish my writing in there. I would eliminate all of those things that are keeping me from being creative and passionate about my writing."

Realistically, he was never going to build an actual shack in his backyard. I said, "Since you can't build a real shack, what is keeping you from creating that very same shack right here in this space?"

The thought had never occurred to him that the space he was working out of could become the ideal space for his writing.

As we worked through his belongings and purged what he didn't need for his current writing projects, he sometimes had a hard time deciding if he should let go of an item.

When that happened I said, "If you had built the shack in your backyard, would you have carried that item out there?" More often than not, he said, "No, I wouldn't want to clutter up the shack with this." He was now able to answer his own question as to whether or not to keep each item.

Look around your home and start keeping those items that help you reach your goals.

If they aren't helping you reach those goals then they're probably keeping you from reaching them. You can create your very own shack filled with those items that are important to you in the life you are living now, if you are willing to let go of the habit of keeping things.

CHAPTER 17

Don't Waste Time on Clutter

In today's world, getting organized is a big topic of discussion. Read the headlines on the magazine covers as you stand in the grocery store line. You'll see plenty of articles related to getting more organized.

Recently, I read two articles that didn't make a lot of sense to me.

The first article was titled, "How to organize your clutter." My first thought was, "Why teach someone how to organize clutter?"

First, let's take a look at what the word clutter means. The definition in the dictionary is, "a large amount of things that are not arranged in a neat or orderly way; a crowded or confused mass or collection, to make a place untidy or overfilled with objects; a condition of disorderliness or overcrowding."

The two words that resonated with me when looking at the definition were overfilled and crowded. People are filling up their homes with items they no longer use, which ends up becoming clutter. When things start to feel overwhelming, they feel the need to organize this excess.

> "Happiness is a place between too little and too much."
>
> ~Finish Proverb

It's actually quite easy to organize items that have now become clutter; putting books in order by the author's last name, boxing up magazines according to year, and stacking plastic bowls by size.

But does it make sense to organize things you no longer need? You can have nicely labeled bins filled with clutter, but why do this? You take time categorizing it, shopping for bins, boxing it up, labeling it and finding a place to stack it. Why do this for things that have lost their meaningfulness?

You end up spending a lot of time rearranging the clutter throughout your home on a regular basis. Weekends are spent organizing clutter only to repeat the process at a later date. All you're doing is shuffling items from space to space, instead of making good decisions on what you really need to keep.

If you're spending too much time organizing the clutter in your home, it's time to break this habit.

With every item in your home ask yourself, "Do I really use this item or am I just in the habit of keeping it?"

Before you bring something new into your home ask yourself, "Is this worth the time I will spend dealing with it?" In other words, "Do I want to spend my free time dealing with items I won't use, or would I rather be doing something more enjoyable and significant with my time?"

Stop organizing clutter even if you have plenty of space in your home to store it. Set guidelines for what you need to keep and let go of the rest. Surrounding yourself with only the items you use and love will free up time to spend with loved ones.

The second article I read was titled, "Ship your clutter to us and we'll store it for you." If storing clutter in your own home doesn't make sense, why would you pay to ship it and incur a monthly fee to store it? If you can live without it on a regular basis, do you truly need it?

Excess clutter rarely makes you happier. Once your basic needs are met, additional items lose their 'happy' value as they become just another thing lying around your home.

CHAPTER 18

An Organized Home is Easier to Move

If you're considering moving to a new home, now is the time to start organizing.

As a former real estate agent, I know first-hand that an organized home sells faster than a cluttered home. If you want to get top dollar and increase the odds your home will sell faster, take time to organize before putting your home on the market.

One of the biggest selling features for home buyers is a home with lots of storage. Every closet, cabinet, pantry and storage space needs to be free of excess items. When potential home buyers look at these spaces, they should look just as inviting as the rest of the home. Not cram-packed with an avalanche of stuff spilling out and falling onto the floor.

Start by organizing the storage areas first. Donate, sell and throw away items you no longer need. Make closets look spacious and storage spaces appear larger. This will not only help you sell your home, but will make it easy for you to find things now.

Once the storage areas have been purged, take a look at all rooms in your home. Cut down on the amount of trinkets and extra furniture in each space. By parting with extras, your rooms will look more welcoming. This will also make it easier to clean up quickly for showings.

> "You spend the first part of your life accumulating stuff and the second half getting rid of it."
>
> ~Unknown

Don't be tempted to box up items from these rooms and put them in your storage areas. Many times these boxes get moved from home to home without ever getting opened. Break this cycle and start letting go of the stuff you're no longer using. Many of these items served their purpose at a time when you needed them, but are no longer necessary for the lifestyle you are currently leading.

Having an organized home sends the message that you also maintain your home properly, which is important to prospects. You will be able to maintain your home better when extra items are not in your way or concealing unexpected issues, such as a leak underneath a cabinet or insects hiding from view.

You'll spend less time and money if you have fewer items to take to your new home. Moving companies charge by weight. Don't pay to move stuff you won't use again. If it's a do-it-yourself move, you'll be able to rent a smaller truck.

Imagine moving into your new home with just the items you need. Not only will it be easier to unpack once you arrive, but your new home will be less cluttered, making it easier to clean and maintain. Stick with your new habit of eliminating excessive stuff. Your daily life and future moves will be far less complicated.

LORI FIRSDON

CHAPTER 19

Get Back to Basics in the Kitchen

The other day at our family cookout, my brother walked up to me holding his plate of food and asked, "Where are your corn holders for the corn on the cob?" To which I replied, "I don't have any."

Even though we are well into adulthood, my brother and I like to tease one another, so I knew the conversation couldn't just end there. He raised his eyebrows and said, "How am I supposed to eat my corn then?" Putting my hands on my hips, I replied, "Real men use their fingers."

Giving this some thought he said, "What if I burn my fingers?" I countered, "I have burn cream in my first-aid kit."

As he walked away, I thought, "I wonder if my kids even know what corn holders are."

Many years ago, I went through my entire kitchen and began purging items that I rarely used and could live without. The corn holders fell victim to this purge.

In my newly organized kitchen, my drawers were no longer crammed with gadgets, and things no longer toppled down from upper cabinets.

I purchased these extra gadgets because I love to cook and thought they would make my life easier. However, getting back to the basics allowed me to find the items I use on a regular basis more quickly with less hassle.

I rarely miss the items I let go of and manage just fine without them.

The other day my youngest daughter made Mickey Mouse pancakes using just a spoon. She doesn't know I used to own a Mickey Mouse pancake mold.

> "Simplicity boils down to two steps:
>
> Identify the essential.
>
> Eliminate the rest."
>
> ~Leo Babauta

I steam delicious rice using a standard pot with a lid instead of the rice steamer that took up space in my pantry.

I laugh when my kids marvel over someone else's melon balls. Since I don't own a melon baller, my kids have always eaten their melon sliced and served on the rind. With five kids, this momma doesn't have time to fuss over a melon.

If you love your gadgets and use them regularly, keep them.

If you feel overwhelmed and cramped in your kitchen, then I suggest you go through each drawer, cabinet and your pantry, and let go of the extras that keep you from using your kitchen efficiently.

Don't worry about how much money you spent on the gadgets or who gave them to you. If you don't use them, they are in your way.

I love kitchen gadgets, so I know firsthand how hard it can be to part with them. If you are unsure if you can live without something, place it in a box and store it away from your kitchen. Label the box with a future date that lets you know when it will be safe to donate the items inside.

If you find you miss using something, pull it from the box and place it back in your kitchen. Those items deserve to be there.

Our next family dinner will be a Mexican theme. I'll have to remember to call my brother and tell him to bring his taco stand. I will not have the patience to hold his taco while he fills it.

CHAPTER 20

Be Prepared for the Next Crisis

We will all face many crises during our lifetime. Some will strike at unpredictable times, like an accident or sudden death of a loved one. Others are planned, like when you invite friends to stay overnight knowing full well the room they will be staying in is buried in clutter. Still others are inevitable, like tax day and you haven't a clue where all the necessary paperwork is to file your taxes.

Whether the crises are large or small, planned or unplanned, getting organized now will help you be better prepared for them.

Getting your paperwork and important documents labeled and filed is a good place to start. Your loved ones should be able to locate the necessary paperwork they need to take care of things should you be hospitalized.

Filing these documents ahead of time not only allows your loved ones to locate things quickly, but will also ensure they have more time to spend with you during your hospital stay.

Having your paperwork in order is also important in the event of your sudden death. During times like this, loved ones are grieving and exhausted. They may also have a hard time concentrating, so having your affairs in order will help them during this difficult period.

Once you get your paperwork in order, show your loved ones where documents are stored, so they can act quickly when necessary.

Suppose you get your paperwork in order but don't fall ill or die anytime soon.

> **"If you want to make an easy job seem mighty hard, just keep putting off doing it."**
>
> **~Olin Miller**

Fortunately, you'll get to reap the benefits of your organizing for many years to come. Knowing where your paperwork is kept gives you a sense of calm and allows you to find things quickly. Finding a receipt to return a purchase, locating the title to the car you just sold or even filing your taxes won't be so daunting.

Next, look for items in your home you no longer have a use for and donate them. Many times the spare bedroom in your home collects clutter because it's an easy catch all. It's easier to toss items in the room and forget about them instead of making decisions on what to do with them.

Lack of decision making is often the reason why people are disorganized. Decide now what your goals are in life and set guidelines for what you need to keep so you'll have less to deal with when crises occur.

By letting go of unnecessary items, you can have a room ready for unexpected guests instead of a junk room that weighs you down every time you think about it. It also provides a great space for you to enjoy when you're not entertaining guests. You'll have a quiet place to relax or the perfect place to work on a project.

People often tell me they don't have time to get organized. Start today by limiting what you bring into your home so you can take time to focus on the items you already own. Commit to spending just a little time everyday going through your home and eliminating the unnecessary. When you can find things faster, you'll gain that time spent organizing back in the long run.

Organizing now will leave you and your loved ones better prepared to deal with any crisis. If you read the chapters in Part One, where my family had to function without me while I had the flu, you saw how being prepared was advantageous in getting through the week.

If you're blessed and not in the midst of a medical crisis, you'll live a more relaxed and peaceful life during the more quiet periods in-between crises.

CHAPTER 21

It's Time to Get Real with Your To-Read Stack

If you're like many people, you have plenty of unread reading material piling up in your home and office. Holding on to this long term can have its disadvantages.

These unread materials easily get mixed in with other paperwork, making it difficult to locate important documents when you need them. It creates health risks by collecting dust, which produces poor air quality and creates a fall risk if left on the floor. It takes up space that might be better used for something else. If you think about it, seeing it piled up probably makes you feel bad.

You may feel guilty for spending money on magazines still in the wrapper many months later, or overwhelmed when you look at the stacks. Is this unread material really worth keeping?

When it comes to unread magazines and other reading material, we often live in our fantasy life which says, "I am going to have time to read everything that enters my home and office." For most of us, our reality is we'll never have time to read everything that crosses our desk, so now it's time to get real.

> "Eliminating clutter gives you room to think."
>
> ~B. Ballinger

When organizing your space, collect all of your unread magazines and reading material into one area. Now ask yourself, "How many minutes a day do I read?" Then ask, "How much of this can I get through if I'm reading that amount of time on a daily basis?"

What's the worst thing that would happen if you let go of most of it right now? I'm guessing you would continue to get more current information delivered to you, or you could go to the internet and locate the information when you need it.

Once you pare down to what you realistically have time to read, don't leave it on your kitchen counter or on your desk unless that is where you actually read. Instead put it in the places where you are more likely to get through it; next to your favorite chair in the family room, on your nightstand, in the bathroom, or in the car to be read while you wait for your child's sporting practice to end.

To keep the clutter from piling up in the future, set some guidelines. One guideline might be, "I will only keep two months' worth of magazines and part with any unread ones when the new issue arrives." Or, "I will only keep enough reading materials that fit into this box. Once it's full I'll read or part with something instead of creating a second box."

Remember, even free magazine subscriptions can take up space, create dust and get in your way. It's time to get real and get selective about what reading materials you allow into your life. If you focus on what you'll gain by letting them go, a more organized and cleaner space, you'll quickly realize how these unread materials could be holding you back from doing the things that really matter.

CHAPTER 22

Old Family Photos
Don't Bring Everyone Joy

At my recent organizing seminar, one of the attendees raised her hand and asked, "When my parents passed away, my siblings gave me the responsibility of all the family photos, since I was the oldest child.

Overnight, I inherited many boxes of photos that were in disarray. I have no interest in most of them. Do I have to keep them?"

My reply was, "Absolutely not." She immediately smiled and thanked me for giving her the answer she needed to hear.

She then asked, "What do I do with them?" My advice was to let her siblings and other family members know she no longer wants the responsibility of storing the photos, then give them a deadline for when they need to pick them up. If they don't make arrangements to get them, she was free to let them go.

After the deadline, she had a few options. If she felt comfortable giving them away, she could offer them to the historical society or antique shops, since some of the photos were very old. After that, it was perfectly fine to shred or discard the photos.

> "Spend more time making memories and less time preserving them."
>
> ~Organize Magazine

After reading this, some of you are relieved by receiving permission to let go of photos you have felt responsible for, while others are in a panic I would even suggest discarding them.

If you are in the latter group, please realize that many people are feeling overwhelmed in their cluttered homes. They need to start taking care of their own needs and organize their homes, so they can start to bring some peace to their lives.

The best way to achieve a more organized home is to keep the things you love and need, not items someone else thinks you should save.

You have to choose how to spend your time. Do you want to make more memories or preserve past ones? For me, camping with my family and friends is much more important than scrapbooking photos of past camping trips.

To any of you who need permission to let go of burdensome photos, I give you permission without a guilt trip. Let them go, and then spend time on what really matters to you.

CHAPTER 23

Children Need Structure in Addition to Love

In my line of work as an organizer, I come across some distressing situations. Children living in hoarding conditions are some of the most heartbreaking. My heart goes out to the parent and the child because the situation is agonizing for both.

I have compassion for the parent because they love their child and want to do the best for them, but their hoarding addiction leaves them feeling paralyzed and powerless. They struggle emotionally to make the necessary changes in order to have a more calm and orderly home.

When I speak with the children, they tell me they feel trapped and want to escape. They describe their home as a warehouse or worse, a junk yard.

Children are embarrassed to have friends over because they don't want them to see the living conditions in their home. They tell me they have plenty of toys, but no one to share in the fun.

Teenagers tell me they do everything they can to stay away from their home. They say, "I can't wait until I am old enough to get far away from this house."

Personally, it gives me a sense of security when my teens are home during their down time. It saddens me to think some teens avoid their home and family because of the clutter.

> "Freedom is the act of releasing ourselves from the bondage of that which keeps us from living the life we were meant to live."
>
> ~Kelli Wilson

The children enjoy being with their parent, but the disarray in the home causes frustration and arguments. The parent/child relationship suffers, and kids temporarily escape to their friends' homes.

In addition to the breakdown of their relationship, there are other concerns for children living among clutter.

Their schoolwork can suffer. They have a difficult time getting ready in the morning and show up late to school, sometimes without breakfast. Children desire structure, so it can be challenging to complete homework among the chaos at home.

Teachers also report homework is often late, lost or forgotten when children live in an extremely disorganized home. Parents also forget to turn in permission slips and other important documents concerning their children.

There are health and safety concerns in a home where hoarding takes place.

Keeping the home clean is difficult because there are too many items to clean around. Children's respiratory conditions are exacerbated because of dust and mold in the home. They require additional medications and breathing treatments to help make breathing easier.

If the kitchen is in endless chaos, it's difficult to prepare healthy meals and keep the kitchen clean. Children are eating less nutritious meals in kitchens that are not sanitary.

If you are a parent who is keeping more items in your home than you can manage, please consider seeking help. Your children love you, but they also feel paralyzed and powerless living in a home with no organization or calmness.

If you are a child who is living with a hoarding parent seek help from a trusted adult. You can also visit childrenofhoarders.com for information and to talk with a professional.

Don't let a cluttered home keep you from having a terrific relationship with your child and a safe, comfortable home. Change your emotional mindset, and then do the physical work necessary to make changes in your home.

Seek the services of professionals if you can't do it alone.

CHAPTER 24

Seniors, Get Organized
Your Safety Depends On It

Many older adults want to continue to be self-sufficient and remain living in their homes during their golden years. However, many seniors are living in unsafe conditions that may prevent them from doing so.

Getting your home organized is an important step to ensure you can continue to live a safe, healthy and independent life.

According to the Centers for Disease Control and Prevention, one in every three adults age 65 and older falls each year. Falls are the leading cause of both fatal and non-fatal injuries.

Many of these falls can be prevented by reducing the clutter you have in your home.

Start clearing the areas where you walk the most. Walkways, hallways and stairs should be free of clutter and well lit.

Continue through your home clearing the clutter from the rooms you use most often to the ones you use the least.

Removing excess clutter from your home will make it easier to keep it clean. Reducing dust in your home can lessen allergies and other respiratory conditions.

> "You are young and useful at any age if you are still planning for tomorrow."
>
> ~Unknown

Attack the storage areas, such as the basement and attic. Many times these areas are great hiding places for insects and rodents. They also conceal maintenance issues, such as leaks, which create conditions for mold and mildew to develop.

All the areas of your home should be accessible

in the event of an emergency. Every second matters in a crisis. Make sure medical personnel can reach you quickly with all of their equipment.

If you organize while you are healthy, your loved ones will be able to take better care of you and your home if you require hospitalization in the future.

Having items stacked too high in your home is dangerous. Items piled high can fall on you, trapping you beneath. Nothing in your home is that important for you to take this risk.

As we age, our balance can become compromised. Keep items you use often in easy to reach locations. This reduces the necessity of using a step stool and possibly falling.

Review your medications and dispose of those that have expired or you no longer use. Excess medications increase the risk of accidental poisonings both for you and children who visit your home. Look for safe drug drop-off programs in your community.

Clear out expired foods from your cabinets, pantry and refrigerator. Eating unsafe food can cause illness, hospitalization and even death.

Make room for foods that will keep you healthy.

As you organize, think about how you want to spend the rest of your life. Write down a few goals. You can focus on keeping the items that help you reach those goals, while creating a safe home.

Some of your goals may be to travel, spend more time with your grandkids, move to a smaller home, or take up a new hobby.

When making decisions about your stuff, ask yourself, "Does this item help me reach my goals?" If it doesn't, it could very well be keeping you from reaching them.

Get your home organized while you're healthy and capable of making smart decisions. If you become ill or need to downsize in a hurry, having an organized home will make it easier for everyone involved.

CHAPTER 25

Grandma's Gift-Giving Can Cause Difficulty at Home

In my parenting class, we talk about children not being able to clean their rooms because they have too many toys. Invariably, a parent will raise their hand and say, "I agree! My child has too many toys, but I can't stop their grandma from buying more."

The room then erupts with other parents chiming in with the same complaint.

So Grandmas, this article is for you. It's meant to say what your daughter-in-law is afraid to tell you or what your daughter has told you repeatedly, but you haven't taken her seriously.

I know grandmas don't want to hear this, but as an organizer, I see the problems that too much gift-giving causes.

When children have too many toys, it's hard for them to be responsible in caring for them. Children often leave toys lying around the house because they know if something breaks, grandma will buy more.

Their toys spill over into every room in the home. The toy clutter affects everyone who lives there. This causes stress and arguments between family members.

The harmony in the home is disrupted because children can't clean their rooms. It's impossible when they have too many toys and not enough space.

"Perhaps too much of everything is as bad as too little."

~Edna Ferber

A room in disarray often starts an argument between parent and child. The parent will yell at the child for not having a tidy room, which often brings tears from the child.

Next thing you know, the other parent is involved and they start arguing. It goes something like this: Wife says, "I have asked your mother to stop buying so many gifts, but she won't listen. You need to tell her to stop."

Husband doesn't want to hurt his mother's feelings, so he says nothing to her. Saying nothing gets him in hot water with his wife.
Now mom and dad are not getting along. That's not good for the children.

It doesn't stop there. Daughter-in-law now resents grandma, and this relationship becomes strained. Sometimes grandma doesn't realize this because the daughter-in-law doesn't want to confront her.

As you can see Grandma, too many toys can create a messy room, a cluttered home, stress, arguments between family members and in some cases, resentment towards you.

So what else can you do to show your love?

Take their ordinary day and make it extraordinary. Bring them lunch at school, take them for ice cream after their sports practice or invite their friends to your home for pizza and movie night.

Giving your grandchildren the gift of your time is the best gift of all. Having the patience to teach them something, like baking cookies, will be treasured long after they outgrow the plastic toys.

If you can't spend time with them because you live too far away, there are plenty of clutter-free options. For example, you can pay for a class or camp the child has an interest in.

Before buying anything, ask the parents for suggestions and honor their wishes.

Showing love is not about how many gifts you buy. It's about spending time with grandkids and buying only the items they really need. It's about respecting that parents know what is best for their family.

Make sure you're adding to their happiness not creating tension. After all, that has been your intention all along.

CHAPTER 26

You Still Have Time to Give the Perfect Gift

The holidays are upon us and you still need gifts for people on your list. They are probably still on your list because they don't need another trinket for their home or piece of clothing in their closet. However, you still want to get them something to show them how much you love and appreciate them. The good news is you may not have to rush out last minute in order to present your loved one with the perfect gift. This year think clutter-free gifts.

One of the best things you can give someone is the gift of time, your time. Listen to what they talk about and you will soon discover many things they need.

Have you heard someone mention how bad they feel because their photos are disorganized and thrown in boxes all over their home? Why not offer to help them with this project as your gift to them?

You could label the photos and sort them by date as they clue you in on that information. Help them with this project this year, and for next year's holiday you'll have a great gift to buy, photo albums to display their newly organized photos. After reading this, aren't you thinking this would be the perfect gift for someone to give you? Tell them. They may be struggling to come up with a good gift idea.

If you're skilled with computers offer to help friends and family with theirs. Not everyone knows how to install the latest security software,  organize photos, make computers operate faster or find the right software to help them with projects. You take it for granted because working with computers comes easy to you, but this would be such a valuable gift for many.

What skills do you have that others struggle with? Working on projects with loved ones will help educate them and give you a chance to spend quality time together.

> "The best present is presence."
>
> ~Unknown

Kids are more likely to remember experiences than the plastic toys given to them every year. This year offer to bring them lunch at school, enjoy a cooking class together, take them roller skating or rent a bounce house and invite all the neighbor kids.

For the teenagers on your list, concert tickets, movie passes, gift cards for fast food and e-books make good choices for those with limited cash. For experiences, treat both of you to a manicure/pedicure or tickets to a sporting event and go to their favorite restaurant afterwards. If they drive, fill up their car with gas while you're out.

You don't have to walk the mall to find the perfect gift this year. Find out the person's interests and see if you can join them. You pay the fees involved, while they get to do what they love. Find out what's keeping them up at night and see if you can help them by taking a chore off their to-do list. Focus on experiences, not stuff, and you'll build memories that will far outlast anything found in a box.

CHAPTER 27

Gift Exchange Not Fun? Stop the Cycle

Have you ever opened a present, smiled a big smile and thanked the person who gave it to you while thinking to yourself, "I don't really want this."?

As I help people organize their homes, I often find these gifts stashed away in the backs of closets or sitting on a shelf in the basement. And many times when we uncover them, my client will roll their eyes and tell an unfavorable story about the gift.

There are stories like: "My mother-in-law bought me those casserole dishes. She's always buying me cooking items even though she knows I don't like to cook. When I open her presents, I feel like I'm not good enough for her son."

Or, "My friend gave me that book knowing I don't like to read. It makes me angry to think I took so much time to pick out a gift that I knew she would enjoy and she didn't even consider what my interests are. I feel like she bought me something she wanted me to have instead of something I would enjoy."

While gift giving and receiving should be something that brings us joy, often it's causing some very angry and hurt feelings.

"It's not what's under the tree that matters most, it's who's around it."

~Unknown

If this is how you feel, stop the gift-giving cycle. Tell the people in your life that gift giving and receiving is no longer important to you. You would rather spend your time and money building relationships and enjoying experiences.

This is often not as difficult as you might think. Many times the other person has been thinking the same thing, but didn't know how to tell you.

Several years ago when it was my turn to host Christmas, I announced that we would be playing games instead of exchanging gifts. This was a bit of a shock, but everyone agreed to give it a try.

The evening was filled with laughter and a shared togetherness. I learned so much about my family members that I don't get to see often. Even the little ones didn't miss the gift exchange.

We have now made this a tradition. I'll never tire of watching my family members act like fools as we play charades.

I also shared with my friends I would no longer be buying gifts for their birthdays. I would instead take them to lunch or dinner. I get to do this twice a year with each friend because now that's my gift from them.

If gift-giving is more about buying something because you feel you have to, or if the gifts you receive cause emotional pain, stop doing it. Tell others you no longer want to spend your time on things. Instead of shopping, toting gifts, wrapping, standing in line at the post office and returning or storing unused gifts, you are going to spend your time on experiences.

If your relationship is a strained one, exchanging gifts and offering a phony display of appreciation is not going to bring you closer and can actually be doing more harm than good.

If you love gifts, then exchange them. If not, don't. It really is that simple.

Summary

Begin Your Clutter-Free Journey

According to an article in the US News and World Report, "The average American spends one year of their life looking for lost or misplaced items."

Looking for items is not only time-consuming, but frustrating. This is not the way you want to spend a year of your life. Earn your time back by reducing the number of things you own so you have less items to look through.

Think about each of your belongings and how they fit into the big picture. Something that brings about a positive feeling can also bring up negative feelings when you think about its overall impact.

Getting started can be difficult. Use what you have learned so far to help you move towards your goals.

A quick way to begin is by stopping clutter before it finds its way into your home. Ask friends and family members to stop buying gifts and start planning experiences instead.

Let go of fear and start making decisions. A wrong decision can be more freeing than no decision at all.

Stop wasting time organizing clutter. Let go of it so you can be more prepared in a crisis, move from your home more easily and travel light in life.

Everyone is affected by clutter, from children through seniors. Let go of the things in your home that hinder learning, or create health problems and safety issues.

Goods things in excess, such as too many kitchen gadgets, books and photographs, can be the culprits keeping you from daily happiness.

To help through the sorting process, ask yourself, "What's the worst thing that will happen if I let go of this item?"

Define success for yourself and start the journey towards the life you want to lead.

Part Three

Time to Organize

Whenever you hear yourself say, "Someday I'll get more organized," you need to remember that someday is not a guarantee. Too many of you are feeling overwhelmed and frustrated right now.

Getting organized is about focusing on what will make you happy now, not waiting for a future happiness.

In Part Three, I share some simple solutions you can implement to start the organizing process.

*O*rganizing is not just about having a clean home. It's a way of life. It's feeling more confident as you go about your day.

Organizing is about everything having an assigned space, not that everything is always in its space.

I believe organizing gets easier as you learn to be happy with less.

Search out time to organize, even if that means finding 15-minutes a day. Turn off the TV, stop surfing the internet or gossiping with a friend.

If you live with others who are disorganized, there are a couple chapters you'll find helpful in this section. A key step to getting others organized is to focus on getting yourself organized first so you can set the example for others to follow.

When it comes to couples working together, 'Happily Ever After' is more important than letting stuff come between you.

Be patient with yourself and others as you work towards an organized life. Things didn't get disorganized overnight, so don't expect they will be fixed overnight.

Read this final section to see if you can find the one nugget that encourages you change in ways you thought impossible.

CHAPTER 28

Think Like a Backpacker When You Organize Your Home

I just finished reading a book about backpackers who trek through the wilderness on the Pacific Coast Trail. Many of them spend months on the trail surviving with only the items in their packs, along with essentials they acquire in various towns along their journey.

When a person takes to the trail, they are very cautious about the weight in their packs. I learned from the book that they will do things like break the handle off their toothbrush and burn chapters from the books they are reading as they finish them, in an effort to lighten their load.

They constantly think about what items are essential and eliminate those that no longer help them reach their next milestone. For example, when they have made it through the snowy part of a trail, they will donate their pickaxe and ice cleats in a special box for other backpackers to use on their trek through the snow.

When I finished the book, a few thoughts came to me. Why don't we live our lives more streamlined with just the essentials we need for the life we are living right now? Why do we save everything from our past milestones and burden ourselves with them throughout our lives?

Backpackers don't continually accumulate stuff and strap on additional backpacks loaded with unnecessary items. This would prohibit them from getting to hike the next part of their journey, and they wouldn't reach the goals they have set for themselves.

So, why do we buy more storage containers, shelves and furniture to store so many things from our past experiences? We then spend our time moving these items from place to place around our homes. We even spend our weekends reorganizing this stuff instead of doing something we enjoy.

Many of you are not reaching the goals you have set for yourself, because you are not carefully considering what you are storing in your backpacks, a.k.a. your homes.

Before you touch your first item, sit back and write down what you want the next part of your life to look like. Who do you want to spend time with, what experiences do you want, what makes you happy?

Now think like a backpacker. Look around your home and see what is extra weight. You have many things you've treasured. They served their purpose when you needed them, but now they are just that, extra weight. These extras look like treasures, but they rob you of your time.

Backpackers have a kind of brotherhood. They help one another in many ways. They are quick to let go of items they no longer need knowing someone else will benefit from their kindness.

> "The more you own the more it owns you."
>
> ~Nicholas Sparks

In the book, one hiker found a ski pole left behind by a fellow hiker, which helped her navigate the snow. Because of her lack of experience she didn't think to bring one. Thanks to a stranger, her life on the trail was made easier with this simple gift. What can you donate that may be useful to someone else?

Your life is a journey, always changing with your age, the people you meet and life's circumstances. Letting go of your stuff should coincide with your life journey.

As the backpacker who reaches his destinations has to stop and reevaluate his belongings, so do you.

CHAPTER 29

No Excuses, Get Organized in This New Year

Getting organized is on many New Year's resolution lists, but some of you are looking around your homes and struggling with how to get started.

Start by writing down all the excuses you have used in the past for why you have been unsuccessful in organizing your home.

Now think like an organized person. They don't let excuses, such as a small home, messy spouse, or lack of fancy organizing products, keep them from being organized.

If you're disorganized, moving into a larger home may not solve your problem. In fact, you may find you are just as disorganized, if not more, because you're taking your disorganization into a larger space.

An organized person takes the space given them and formulates a plan needed to get organized. For example, over Christmas break we went on a cruise. The room was small, especially with four of us sharing the space.

> "If you really want to do something you'll find a way. If you don't, you'll find an excuse."
>
> ~Jim Rohn

Upon entering our room, we agreed to divide the room into equal parts to help us keep track of our belongings. Each person would use one drawer, a closet shelf, a few hangers and a space on the shelf under the bathroom sink for our cosmetic bags.

Even though we were cramped for space, our room stayed organized because of the few simple guidelines we put in place at the beginning of our stay.

Do away with the excuse that you can't be organized because those around you are not. You can live with a disorganized person and still be organized yourself.

Look for spaces that are solely in your control and organize those. Your nightstand, your side of the closet, a bathroom drawer, your purse or wallet and your car are all spaces you can organize even when those around you don't keep their spaces organized.

You'll feel better and find things faster when your spaces are organized. Don't let the fact that the rest of your home isn't organized the way you would like it to be keep you from being organized.

Don't use the excuse that you can't afford expensive organizing products. Let go of the idea that being organized has to cost a lot of money. Being organized is not about having a home that magazine companies want to photograph. It's about being less frustrated when looking for things, and getting out the door on time without feeling stressed and rushed.

Look for inexpensive items you can use to organize your home. Cardboard boxes picked up free from a grocery store or empty shoeboxes you've been storing, and a Sharpie marker would be a great place to start.

Also, look for items you already have in your home that might serve as organizing products. Many years ago when we purchased a refrigerator with an icemaker, I took the ice cube trays we no longer needed and used them to store my earrings. They are not picture perfect, but they work beautifully in my shallow bathroom vanity drawer.

If your home is disorganized, recognize when you are making excuses and come up with solutions instead. If you struggle with this, find someone you know who is organized and ask for their ideas.

When it's time to take action, throw away the excuse list you created. That's the first thing in your way.

CHAPTER 30

Getting Started is the Challenge

Recently I knocked on the door of a woman who called me to help organize her home. As she opened her door to let me in, she suddenly burst into tears. She had not allowed a visitor into her home in many years and was embarrassed for me to see it.

I first met this woman when she attended one of my seminars. Her clothing was pressed, her hair in a designer cut and her nails perfectly manicured. She looked flawless. Now the secret of living in a cluttered home, one she had been keeping from the rest of the world, had been exposed when she opened her door and allowed me to step inside.

Through tearful eyes she said, "I didn't know where to start. It's all so overwhelming. I feel paralyzed when I look around."

If you find yourself in a similar situation, my advice to you is start somewhere. Pick a spot, the kitchen table, the family room couch or your nightstand and focus on that one small space until it's done.

It doesn't matter where you start. The goal is to unlock your perception that you won't have success, which is one of the reasons you feel paralyzed.

By focusing on just one small space at a time, you will have many small successes that will motivate you to continue to the next area.

> "Faith is taking the first step even when you don't see the whole staircase."
>
> ~Martin Luther King, Jr.

Start in one room and break it down into small projects. For example, if you choose to organize your kitchen, start with the kitchen table. Then focus on the counter tops.

Continue with the upper cabinets doing just one at a time as time allows. When those are complete, de-clutter the lower cabinets and any drawers. Get just one cabinet or drawer done without worrying about when you might have time to get to the next one.

Make sure you keep a trash can and donate bin nearby. Make it easy to remove those items you no longer need.

Don't worry if you mess up other rooms in your home as you carry items from the space you are organizing to their proper rooms. You will tackle the rest of the house one small area at time and those items will be put away when you focus in those areas.

Your goal is to get small tasks done on a regular basis instead of feeling anxious and defeated before you ever get started.

If you feel panicked and overwhelmed about where to start, try starting where you're standing. Don't worry about how little you get done or how much more you have to do. Focus on the small task before you, not everything that needs to be done in the whole house. You will feel less paralyzed.

Sometimes action has to come before motivation. Set your overwhelmed feelings aside, roll up your sleeves, and promise yourself you won't let your past failed attempts keep you from one small success at a time. Once you start enjoying the newly organized spaces, you'll be motivated to tackle the next small project.

CHAPTER 31

Start 'Someday' Projects Today

One year, while I was enjoying our hometown's Greek festival, a woman stopped me and said, "I enjoy your articles. I read every one of them." We chatted for a bit, and then it was time to go our separate ways.

As we turned to leave, she said, "Keep up the good work. I promise you, someday I'm going to take all your advice and make the changes I need to do to improve my life." As I walked away, her word 'someday' stuck in my mind.

Here was a woman who went out of her way to let me know the advice I was sharing was valuable to her, but she was not getting her organizing projects started.

Few of us have the time to organize our entire home while letting everything else in our lives go by the wayside. Instead of saying, "Someday I'll do that," see if you can do something today towards your goal to get organized.

> **"The greatest of all mistakes is to do nothing because you can only do a little. Do what you can."**
>
> **~Sydney Smith**

Organizing is a process not an event. Start the process by choosing any space in your home that bothers you the most. Then break it down into small tasks you can accomplish in 15 minutes or less.

If you choose to work in your bedroom, for example, start by organizing just one drawer a day until all the drawers in the room have been purged of the items you no longer need and the remaining items are neatly folded. Work on just the items on top of your dresser or under the bed next.

Or start in your closet and organize just your shoes, pants or short sleeves. Don't worry about the fact that the whole closet isn't done in one session. If you work just 15 minutes a day on each category in your closet, sooner or later your whole closet will be organized.

As each small area gets organized, you will notice that life gets a little bit easier because you'll start finding the things you need faster than before.

Your home will also be easier to clean, and you'll do less shopping because you'll see what you already have. All of this saves time, which gives you the organizing minutes you need to start on the next space.

Wake up every day this week 15 minutes early and start organizing a space. You can leave the house knowing you accomplished your organizing project for the day.

You can also work small organizing projects into your daily life.

Organize the kitchen utensil drawer while waiting on a pot of water to boil. Clean out expired medications from your home while waiting on a family member to get ready to leave the house. Organize your purse while waiting for your child's team practice to end. These are all ways to make use of those minutes that are often wasted doing nothing.

Start anywhere in your home. The kitchen junk drawer, the DVDs, your child's stuffed animals or the old trophies you have boxed up in the basement. Just start somewhere and work for 15 minutes.

Getting your projects done in small, manageable increments will enable you to see progress. The more projects you complete, the more you'll feel motivated to continue to the next one.

CHAPTER 32

A Place for Everything

Our home will never be Better Homes and Gardens picture-ready. Just like other families our mail gets tossed on the kitchen counter, clothes don't make it to the hamper and coats end up on the couch instead of in the closet.

I would love to have a neat and tidy home at all times, but that's unrealistic. It would require me to constantly monitor everyone's actions and correct them at every turn. That's not what I want to do.

However, there does come a time when we have to take the time to get things in our home back in place. If we don't, we waste our time looking for things instead of doing what we enjoy.

Being organized is about paring down to the things you love and need, and assigning a space for every item. "A place for everything and everything in its place," as the saying goes.

You then let everyone in your home know where things belong so when the time comes to straighten up they can.

I discovered the other day that my dog knows that certain items in our home have assigned spaces. Heidi is my running partner. She loves to run with me and always gets excited when it's time to go.

My running clothes are kept in a specific drawer in the armoire in my bedroom. She has never been in my room because we don't allow her to go upstairs, yet she whines and paces around the foyer excited before she sees me wearing my running clothes. She hears the drawer open and knows we'll be running soon.

She also knows the iPod I'll take is downstairs in

my office drawer. She gets over-the-top, super excited when I'm wearing my running clothes and I open that drawer.

Now if my dog knows where certain items are kept in my home, then certainly our spouses and children could be trained in a similar fashion. I realize this sounds a bit condescending, but it's true.

To achieve this, start by standing at the doorway of every room in your home and define the purpose of each room and what items are needed to serve that purpose.

Once you determine the purpose, you will quickly see what items belong in the room and what items need to be removed. Pare down to just the items that belong in the room, then assign each item a specific space.

> **"Don't put it down, put it away."**
>
> **~Unknown**

Let everyone who lives in your home know the purpose of each room and where the items are kept within each room.

If you do this, everyone will be able to retrieve and return items to their rightful place. Even though things won't be put away all the time, it will be easier to straighten up when it's time to 'crack the whip' and get things back in order.

It's really not about having a perfectly organized home at all times. Just strive for a sense of calm and order most days.

Be patient while everyone is learning the newly assigned spaces. You will still get asked at times where something is even though your home is organized. When my loved ones ask where something is and I'm not sure at the moment, my response is simple. "I don't know, but the dog might."

CHAPTER 33

Get Back 55 Minutes a Day by Using a Routine

An article in Newsweek stated, "The average American spends 55-minutes a day looking for things they own, but cannot find."

In addition to this time wasted, there is also frustration and stress that goes with searching for items, which is heightened when you are in a hurry or someone is waiting on you.

Having routines is a great way to lessen these wasted 55-minutes a day.

Start by paying attention to how you waste your time, and see if you can put routines in place to prevent it from happening again.

Some routines I find helpful are:

If you frequent a particular store often, park your car in the same row each time you go.

My youngest daughter often accompanies me to the grocery store. As we were leaving the store one day, she stopped and said, "Where did we park?"

"Lost time is never found again."

~Benjamin Franklin

My first thought was, "Not remembering where you park is not just an old age thing," and secondly, "My daughter has never caught on that I park in the same row every time I visit this grocery store."

That day my daughter learned a routine that mom does consistently to save time. What we didn't know was this would come in handy the very next week.

My husband was ready to take her to soccer practice, but was delayed because they couldn't find her cleats. She suddenly remembered they were still in the trunk of my car from the last practice, but I was at the grocery store.

My husband grabbed my extra set of car keys, drove to the store and was directed to "Mom's" grocery store row by my daughter. They found my car quickly and retrieved her cleats from my trunk.

Having routines in place saved my family time that day. My husband found my spare keys promptly because I routinely hang them on the same hook near our exit door. My daughter found the car easily in a full parking lot, and I didn't have to leave my grocery shopping to assist them.

I have since put a new routine in place. I ask my children to double check that they have all of their belongings out of the car before heading into the house.

Put items used routinely such as your cell phone, keys, purse and wallet in the same location in your home when you're done using them for the day.

Place items that need to be put in the car in a designated location near your door. This will keep you from searching for them when it's time to leave.

Gather paperwork and create folders when you have several papers pertaining to the same subject, instead of leaving them in stacks mixed with unrelated papers. File these folders in a drawer for easy retrieval.

Find a place in your home for every item you own, and routinely return items to their proper place.

The next time you're searching for something, stop and ask yourself, "What solution can I put in place so I won't waste time looking for this again?"

Finding things fast saves time. Every minute saved adds up over the course of a day.

How will you spend your 55-minutes a day you'll gain by having your things in order?

CHAPTER 34

Stop Letting Stuff Get in the Way of Happy Relationships

For those of you who are married, think back to the time when you were excited to move in with one another and start your new life as a married couple. You brought your things into the home and your partner did the same.

Everything was great until one day, one spouse started feeling overwhelmed with the items accumulated in the home and the disorganization that followed. This led to bickering and hurt feelings. Home sweet home started getting lost in the piles of stuff.

There are several things you can do to find balance and live in harmony with someone who may not be as organized as you.

Take care of your items first before worrying about what your spouse is up to. There are many areas of your home you have control over. Organize your closet, sock drawer, bathroom drawer, hobby room, car and any other space that is yours.

You'll feel better and more in control, once you pare down to the items you need and keep them organized. Staying focused on yourself gives you less time to be bothered by your spouse's things and more time to accomplish things that are important to you.

Sometimes couples use stuff as a way to control one another. While working with a client in her craft room, I suggested

> "Promise yourself to spend so much time improving yourself that you have no time left to criticize others."
>
> ~Christian Larsen

she part with some of the items she no longer needed. Her response was, "I won't part with those until my husband parts with the tires in the garage that belong to a car we no longer own."

If you're keeping score like this, you might have a marital concern that should be dealt with before attempting to organize your home.

When you're ready to work together, find a balance. Agree that some rooms will remain orderly, while others can have some degree of disarray. For example, the living room is organized, while the home office stays behind closed doors. The kitchen is her domain, while the garage is his. Marriage is a compromise. Remember this when organizing your home.

While organizing, share your progress with your spouse. When you donate items, let her see how much you parted with. If you sell something, announce how much you earned. If something was particularly hard to let go of, share this too.

We sold our horse a couple years ago, but I wasn't ready to part with my cherished saddle until recently. I was happy when a young girl purchased it, but once she left I looked at my husband and said, "I think I might cry." He hugged me and said, "It went to a good home." I was comforted by his words, even though he was probably smiling over my head knowing we would never pay for the upkeep of another horse.

When one spouse is trying hard to improve the household organization, I often see the other spouse jump on board and start organizing too. Soon after I sold my saddle, my husband was ready to part with his childhood coin collection.

When working with your spouse, be patient and strive for progress, not perfection. When arguments arise, remember what's important. Stop letting stuff get in the way of a happier marriage.

CHAPTER 35

Don't Let Extra Items
Sneak into Your Home

A mother from my daughter's school pulled me aside the other day to share a story that recently happened to her.

She told me she had been struggling for some time to get organized while working full-time and raising four children. She decided to go to the library to get an organizing book to look for tips on getting her home organized.

When it was time to return the book she couldn't find it. She lost the organizing book she borrowed! She had to pay the library for the replacement. We shared a good laugh and then she said, "Because of my limited time, I can't do any major organizing projects right now. I'm just trying to keep my head above water. Do you have any tips on what I can do differently?"

Many ideas came to mind, but I knew I had to give her something manageable to start with, or she would feel too overwhelmed to do anything.

> **"You don't have to organize what you don't bring in."**
>
> **~Unknown**

If you are struggling with a disorganized home and have little time to organize like this mother, start by monitoring what items you bring into your home. Only bring those items in that are necessary. By doing this, you'll have fewer unnecessary items to deal with later, which will give you more time to catch up on what's already made it into your home.

Items sneak into our homes in many ways. Often times these items are free so we take them. I am constantly turning away freebies that I know will someday waste my time.

Here is an example of how easily extra items can make their way into my home.

Every year my church provides new calendars to their parishioners. After church one day, I turned toward the exit doors and saw all five of my young children with a calendar in hand. I instantly turned five children around and had them return the calendars. I knew my children would not use the calendars and they would be scattered about my home long forgotten. If you feel like you can't handle another thing, stop yourself and your loved ones from taking things you really don't need. No more free pens, canvas shopping bags, coffee mugs or water bottles. Don't subscribe to free magazines unless you're reading the ones you already have.

Stop taking plastics shopping bags when you can carry an item or two from the store without one. When free make-up items are offered to you because you reached a certain sales quota, only take those products you will really use and leave the rest at the store.

How about those hand-me-downs well-meaning friends continue to give you even though your children's rooms are bursting with excess? Take only those items you need and have them pass the rest to someone else.

Once you stop taking in unnecessary items, you will gain time to purge and donate the excessive items you currently own.

Get used to saying, "No thank you." when people want to hand you something.

The next time you reach for a free item ask yourself, "If I had to pay for this, would I take it?" Chances are if you wouldn't pay for it you don't need it.

CHAPTER 36

Daily To-Do List
Eases Strain on the Brain

Talk with any organized person and chances are they routinely jot things down on to-do lists instead of trying to remember the tasks they have to get done. Organized people don't trust their memory, they trust their lists.

If you stop to think about, what you think about, it's often the many things you have to get done. We spend a lot of our brain power remembering and reminding ourselves of the many tasks we have to do.

Writing things down, instead of keeping them on your mind, frees your mind to think about other more creative things. You can relax knowing what you have to get done is written down and can be referred to when you're ready to tackle a task on your list.

The first step in maintaining an efficient to-do list is to keep things written down in one system, instead of making many lists. Multiple lists tend to get scattered around your home and office. Some suggestions to keep your lists together: use a three-ring binder, index cards attached with a ring or electronically in your phone.

Once you decide on a system for capturing your tasks, break your list into various lists within that system based on what it is you need to do. If you have errands to run, start a list titled errands. For your calls, title one phone calls. Other categories you may want to consider are home repairs, grocery, specific retail stores, books you want to read or ideas for a project you're working on.

> "The discipline of writing something down is the first step towards making it happen."
>
> ~Lee Iacocca

By breaking your to-do list into various

categories, you will only look at the information you need when you need it. When making your calls, you won't be looking at the errands you need to run and so on. Looking at specific lists saves time.

To decide which list a task should go on, think about what needs to be done first in order to complete each task. For example, if your car needs an oil change, write that on your call list so you can make an appointment, or put it on your errand list if you plan to stop in a shop that doesn't require appointments.

If you call for an appointment, check your call list and see what other calls you can make while you're sitting with your phone and calendar in hand. When you go for your oil change, check your errand list and see what other errands you can accomplish while in that area. You'll save time by getting similar tasks completed back-to-back.

Keep your to-do list nearby so you can write down tasks as they surface. Breaking your list down by various categories will help you accomplish similar tasks quickly.

Writing things down frees your mind from the never ending remembering and reminding cycle. You'll feel less stressed knowing you have a compiled list ready for when you have the time to accomplish your necessary tasks.

Give your brain a break. Write tasks down so your mind can be more relaxed and able to focus on the present moment.

CHAPTER 37

Motivating Housemates to Get Organized

You've decided you want to have a more organized home, but how do you motivate everyone else in your household to jump on board?

If you want others to change, set a good example in the spaces that belong to you. Your master bedroom, master bath and the home office are all spaces you have the most control over.

Many times I'm hired by parents to help organize their homes, and the first place they want to start with is their children's rooms.

I suggest we start in the parents' room because this is the best way to set an example and show children how an organized room can look when we finish. Often the children want their rooms to be next.

Keeping your shoes, coats, car keys and paperwork organized will also set a good example for others to follow.

If your spouse or children have too much stuff, making it impossible for them to organize, it's time to help them downsize.

Before tackling the clutter, it's important to find out what their goals are. Do they want to have more time for hobbies, entertain more, play outside with their friends or do less housework?

> "Clutter is not just the stuff on the floor – it's anything that stands between you and the life you want to be living."
>
> ~Peter Walsh
>
> *It's All Too Much*

Once you find out what their goals are, there's a very good chance that some of the items they are saving will be keeping them from reaching these goals. If they have a difficult time parting with something they no longer use, ask them, "Is this helping you reach your goals?"

Sometimes they don't want to part with something because they think it's valuable. Finding out the true value of the items may be all that is needed for them to part with it.

If an item does have value, offer to help them sell it. Sometimes people are willing to part with something, but doing the legwork of selling it holds them back.

Finding a good home for their stuff may be all it takes for them to part with it. Donating craft supplies to a nursing home, bath towels to an animal shelter or costume jewelry to a school's theater program can be great avenues for items they no longer need. Check the websites of their favorite organizations for wish lists.

Remind the person if they don't deal with their excess now, loved ones will have to at a later date if they become ill or pass away.

Helping others get organized takes patience and understanding. Be compassionate and supportive as they make progress when letting go of their things. Stay positive and congratulate them as they organize each space.

CHAPTER 38

Enjoy Family During Holidays

My job as a professional organizer is to help people make decisions on their physical clutter and inspire them to reach goals that are important to them.

Sometimes I get lucky and clients inspire me.

Several years ago as I was leaving a session, a client expressed how excited she was to have a newly organized home to invite guests into for the holidays, something she hadn't been able to do for many years.

I offered to retrieve her holiday decorations from the attic so she could start decorating. She directed me to one plastic bin and a small tree. I questioned her about where her additional holiday bins were. She said, "That's all I have. I have learned over the years to keep only the decorations that are special." She decided it was more important to spend time with family during the holidays than decorate her home lavishly.

In the bin was a wreath, ornaments her children made, a candy dish her mother painted, a holiday kitchen towel her aunt embroidered and a few angel figurines.

I left her home inspired to make changes so I could spend more time with my family during the holidays.

> "Enjoy the little things in life, for one day you may look back and realize they were the big things."
>
> ~Robert Brault

Changing habits can be difficult, plus I still had young children at home so I knew paring down was going to be a process, not an event.

The first year: I donated any decorations I didn't put up that year. Some had sentimental value, but I decided not to put them back in the box only to store them for another year. Donating lets someone else enjoy them.

Year 2: I reduced the number of Christmas cards I sent out. No more sending cards to people I don't see or talk to throughout the year.

Year 3: I announced to my husband that I no longer wanted to exchange gifts between us. Instead, we could enjoy a date night without kids. This year we dined at a quaint café in town. My husband proposed to me there so it was a special place for us. It's simple, but much more enjoyable than shopping, standing in lines, wrapping and returning wrong sizes.

Year 4: I suggested to extended family that we no longer exchange gifts, but instead do something together as a family. Everyone agreed. One year, we saw a Christmas production at a local dinner theater; another year we stayed in and played games. Another time, we rode the "Polar Express" train in Indiana, pajamas were encouraged.

Year 5: Our daughter picked out one of the smallest trees on the lot. Not quite as bad as Charlie Brown's tree, but close. My first thought was, "What would our guests think about this humble little tree?" After all, we have high ceilings in our living room and could have a much grander tree.

We came home with the little tree. It was less of a fuss to put in the stand, needed less lights, plus she could reach to decorate it all by herself. Small trees are my preference now.

This year: Fewer lights outside. I am only going to light up my favorite tree.

All of these changes over the years have given us more time to enjoy what we love: baking cookies, playing games, taking in holiday movies and relaxing with friends and family.

This holiday season, stop doing the things you think you 'should' do and start doing what's important to you.

Summary

Steps to An Organized Life

Like the backpackers in this last section, you too can learn to travel light. Keep only what you need in your home for the current phase of your life. Anything extra can slow you down and exhaust you as you travel through your days.

Get a pen and paper and answer these few questions to help with making decisions on what to keep and what to let go of, so you can spend more time doing what you love.

1. Moving forward, I want to spend more time with these friends and loved ones:
2. My bucket list contains these activities I still want to experience:
3. Doing these things on a consistent basis makes me happy:

Pay attention to the excuses you tell yourself about why you can't get organized. Excuses leave you powerless. Don't let them have control over you.

Go room by room throughout your home and list the purpose of each area. Remove items that don't coincide with the purpose.

Choose a place to start and take the necessary steps needed to move forward. Small successes will keep you motivated to continue.

As you make decisions on what's important, remind yourself that you don't want to spend your life rearranging and moving things.

Once you find a designated place for something, label the box, shelf or drawer so others will know where to find things, and just as important, where to put things away.

Write to-do items down. Use your mind for creative thoughts, not routine ones.

If you dislike organizing, be vigilant about what you bring home so you don't have to organize it.

Do the emotional and hands-on work necessary to grasp everything you still want to accomplish.

LORI FIRSDON

Conclusion

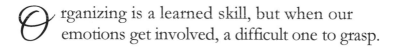rganizing is a learned skill, but when our emotions get involved, a difficult one to grasp.

I hope from reading this book, you are thinking differently about your stuff and motivated to declutter your mind along with your home.

It's human to feel emotions as you walk through your home making decisions on what you keep and part with. Cry when you need to cry. Reminisce. Feel joy. Appreciate the items that served their purpose, but do not let your emotions get in the way of making the changes you desire.

Take time to reflect and let the feelings wash over you, while you prepare to put yourself first and your belongings second.

Fear will be a voice you hear in your head at times. Don't let it be the loudest voice.

As you go through the decluttering process, remind yourself that items are mementoes, not your memories. A memento is something tangible, an item you can hold in your hand and tell a story about. Memories are something you keep with you at all times, without mementoes being present. Close your eyes, put your hand over your heart and feel the memories that reside there as you think about a loved one or a special day.

Mementoes can be given to others, while the memories are yours to treasure.

Focus on what you'll gain by letting go and surround yourself with items that make you happy and support your future plans.

According to the Centers for Disease Control and Prevention, 80% of our medical expenditures are now stress related. We need to find ways to reduce our tension and anxiety to improve our health.

If you are stressed by the overwhelming number of items you own, take a serious look at what you are keeping. Without good health, the things you own won't have much meaning.

Make health and happiness priorities in your life. Happiness comes from experiences because we tend to remember and reminisce about them longer. Focusing on experiences with loved ones and cherished friends will bless you with lasting happiness.

Organizing is about making decisions, not rearranging things. Overcome the emotional attachment to things, treat yourself to happiness and let your personal value system guide you.

As I wrote this summary, I was sitting at a picnic table surrounded by Mother Nature in a campground. This is my perfect way to spend a weekend.

As I wrote these final words, a stray cat unexpectedly came out of the wooded area near me. She looked hungry, but when I approached her she ran back into the woods. I had a can of tuna with me so I opened it and set it near where she had appeared earlier. As I backed away, I called her with a soft, "Kitty-kitty."

She appeared again, smelled the tuna and began frantically eating as if she hadn't eaten recently. I talked gently to her without making a move toward her. Further in the woods, I heard a tiny meow and within seconds her kitten appeared, followed by three more.

The momma cat who had been savagely eating the tuna as fast as she could, backed away and allowed her kittens to finish the can. Never once stopping them so she could eat again. Her selfless gesture warmed my heart.

My tradition when camping is to park the car and not drive it again all weekend until it's time to leave. But that day I veered from my custom and went to buy cat food.

When I returned I lined up five cans near the wooded opening and quietly called them. Momma cat cautiously looked at me then began eating from one of the cans. One by one her kittens found a can and began eating.

I will never forget their tiny purrs as they shared in the mini-feast before them. I felt such gratitude for being witness to their pleasure.

Simple pleasures like this make me happy. This is an experience that will stay on my heart for a long time.

It would not have been possible for me to have this wonderful experience without first, making a goal to camp more often and second, letting go of things that would have kept me from escaping for the weekend.

Think about your perfect weekend. Do the emotional and practical work to de-clutter to achieve your life goals.

ACKNOWLEDGMENTS

I'm an efficiency expert, but human, therefore I cannot escape the grips of procrastination at times. Compiling these articles into a book was something that kept getting pushed to the side. Until one day, my daughter's sixth grade English teacher, Mrs. Horwath, offered to share her expertise and lend a hand with getting me started. Thank you for the much needed push and encouragement.

I'm all about hiring my weaknesses. Since publishing books is not my strength, I turned to Gery Deer, who I met during a networking meeting. His company, GLD enterprises, coaches writers through the book publishing process from start to finish. Thank you for your incredible wisdom and for giving me the confidence to continue with the book.

Designing a book cover was much more challenging than I expected. Fortunately, I had Nola Cooper, who had the vision and patience as we saw this project through. In addition to this book cover, she has been a great support system with other projects. Thank you, Nola, for your talent and dependability over the years.

I owe a huge amount of thanks to Nicole Amsler from Keylocke Services, who came to the rescue when I felt like giving up. Without her, this book never would have come to completion. Nicole's creativity, professionalism and attention to detail were exactly what was needed to help me finally finish this project. I am forever grateful for Nicole's knowledge, skill and quick response.

And finally to my office manager, Amy Klees, who I fondly refer to as 'Amazing Amy' because of her tremendous help in running the business behind the scenes and her help in editing this book. I am grateful to her for everything she does for me and the clients we serve.

ABOUT THE AUTHOR

Lori Firsdon spends her days teaching people how to get organized so they feel more confident and discover peace where there is chaos.

She shares her practical organizing solutions on a personal level with clients and audiences who are looking for ways to make positive changes in their lives.

She is a member of the National Association of Productivity and Organizing Professionals and the National Speakers Association.

When she's not working, she enjoys camping, biking, reading and spending time with her husband, Jim and their five children, Michelle, Erica, Scott, Alex, and Leah and their significant others.

She lives in Dayton, Ohio.

RESOURCES

Lose Your Stuff,
Find Yourself

You will find numerous resources, links, worksheets, and information on the Forte Organizer website.

www.ForteOrganizers.com

While you're there, click on the Resource tab and sign up for our free monthly newsletter. We promise not to clutter up your in-box. Our e-newsletter includes new articles, organizing solutions for your home and office, and information about upcoming seminars, books, and events.

Follow us on social media as well:

www.facebook.com/ForteOrganizers

www.pinterest.com/firsdon

Lori Firsdon helps others take control of their space. She is also available for speaking and consulting nationwide. Details can be found on the website.